www.finishinglinepress.com

To the 4 a.m. Light

poems by

Adrienne S. Wallner

Finishing Line Press
Georgetown, Kentucky

To the 4 a.m. Light

For James -

Thank you for your support, encouragement, and words of inspiration. Hope to work together again some day!

Adrienne S Wallner

April 2021

Publisher: Leah Huete de Maines

Editor: Christen Kincaid

Cover Art: photograph by Adrienne S. Wallner of "Magdalene" by Dessa Kirk

Author Photo: Derrick R. Jaeger

Cover Design: Elizabeth Maines McCleavy

Order online: www.finishinglinepress.com
            also available on amazon.com

Author inquiries and mail orders:
Finishing Line Press
P. O. Box 1626
Georgetown, Kentucky 40324
U. S. A.

Table of Contents

for Philip Richard Stock,
Gerry,
and Chain Lake.

"I stumbled onto bliss. And I have no intention of finding my way back out."
—David Bowie

Apology

You
were right.

It was mostly
my fault.

I didn't
blame you.

I regret
certain things

I did
before you,

certain things
I did

with you.
I always

just wanted
to make things

work.
If I had to

do it
over again,

I wouldn't
do it

at all.
I am sorry

these are
all lies.

Ticket Stub

It was when my stomach
folded into an origami crane
and my eyes poured slowly
from their sockets,
viscous enough to be
spread over stale cakes
and saturate each
to saccharine pulp,
that I removed my Lungs
and placed them in the middle
of the living room floor.
Right Lung was slightly
larger than Left,
I noticed.
Had I panted less with Left?
Had Right been greedily
bellowing in fright and sex,
shoving twin kin aside
with each gasp and heave,
relegating Left to
whispers and hums?
Or was Left just lazy,
only inhaling when I was
dormant and drowsy?
I left my Lungs in the living room
while I made a cup of coffee,
not caring who might step on,
or over, or who would even notice.
I didn't need to breathe anymore.
It weighed me down.
And I was prepared to press on
without Right Lung
or Left Lung
or the insistent nuisance
of respiration.
I sipped my coffee and
poked at my Lungs

with the handle of a spoon—
such a useless mound of tissue.
I think I might fill the hole with
an electric fireplace.
Or perhaps leave it empty
and charge admission.

Night Thaw

Mute blue ice knocks
swells and moans
round hollow whale moans
that ricochet beneath
the surface of Chain Lake.
Glacial gestures melt,
crack, shrink, freeze—
movement by altering
molecular structure.
Movement not seen, but heard.
Groans bend their echoes
bottom up, bouncing thick
waves that grow louder in
the crisp still of darkness.
A bright white moon
alights the uneven,
tirelessly repeated
thaw and freeze.
A great spectral bellow.
A grand, scraping,
beautiful sound of science—
melting motion amplified
tumbling into itself,
reverberating each minute shift.
Bottomless voices mumble bubbles
below drowned growls
and deep creaks that whiplash
between shorelines where
fragile ice edges heave
their length. I close my eyes
and inhale the sonic atmosphere.
I feel the lake lean, crystal edges
crinkling as they reach
into the water between beaches
coaxing the dark body
that speaks these frozen tongues.

Morning

If I were you, I would not expect
breakfast. That is, I will not cook for you. You
can expect something else
from the trained bitches you are
accustomed to, but not in my kitchen.
I am what you might call a natural
animal. I may lay naked across the kitchen
table white and blue checked tablecloth awry
creased and crumpled beneath my
stomach breasts smashed against cold china
plates forks stabbing my thighs my right knee
digging into the butter my left leg splayed over
the table's edge, foot sideways on the bridge
of the chair. I would kiss the lip of your
coffee cup curving a concave cavern of
familiar fixation shaping for an instant
a world you will worship. I would
arch and twist my body—left toes tipping the
chair right leg crushing the bacon backside
spilling the sugar and sending the cream
flowing to trickle on the floor until
I am supine in your pancakes. You will
have to climb over to drink your coffee.

Judith in My Living Room

On David Palladini's Illustration for Werner Herzog's "Nosferatu" Film Poster (1979) & Gustav Klimt's "Judith 1" (1901)

I raged my Crayolas over the bold
outlines of my coloring book. Judith's eyes
gazed lazily at me. She had taken Nosferatu's place
after he was moved into my parents' bedroom. But
Palladini's likeness of Kinski's unforgettable undead
had never scared me. I never knew it should have.
Nosferatu cradled his victim's body with care—
a woman with tumbling tendrils of dark brown hair.
Her dress, both their skins, alabaster white penetrated
by a red sash slashing her waist. His left eye
ever-shifted sideways looking at me. The woman's eyes
stared up at him. I remember staring back into
the inky hollow of Nosferatu's eye, and watching
the red-sailed ship on a sickening green sea float
past the window behind him, wondering
who was on it and where they were going.

I don't remember when or why
Nosferatu was relocated,
but when Gustav Klimt's *Judith I* occupied
the space above the fireplace,
it was as if another mother had moved in.
Judith was tall and strong and bold.
She could not be ignored.
Her left breast unashamedly bare,
right breast obscured by
a blue peignoir, gilded with
Klimt's signature gold curves and curls.
The shadowed softness of
her skin interrupted
by jeweled gold bangles clasping
smooth restriction around her neck.
As I sat cross-legged on the carpet,
Judith fixed her stare on me.

"Look at me," she said. "Know
your beauty," she said.
Her eyelids hung heavy
with exhaustion,
or relief, or conquest.
Left eye, open just enough
to distinguish a pupil.
Eyebrows arched towards seduction,
her lips parted pausing at a whisper,
on the verge of speaking directly to me.
"I am here," she said.
"Where are you?"
She stood before a frozen forest of gold,
her hair, an endless black window to night,
a voluminous crown around her defiant face,
defining her. Triumphant—
natural, wild beauty conquering.
"I am not weak," she said.
"I am not what you ask for."
"I am power."
"I am strength."
"I am beauty."
"I am real."
"I am you."
I looked up to her,
and always answered "Yes."

As I grew into myself and my sex
Crayolas became cigarettes
and Judith followed me
to my first college apartment. The efficiency above
a questionable tattoo parlor. The living room, was the bedroom,
was the entire apartment. There she stood, between
the two windows meeting me at the moment I walked in—
watching me, reminding me, asking me.
"I am here."
"Where

are you?"

In my next apartment, Judith was in my living room
before I even had furniture. She leaned
up against the wall and waited,
until she could be the center of the room.
There, the last hour of sun would
coruscate between the 70's Venetian blinds
and emblazon Judith's skin with thick swaths
of blood orange. Her head tipped back slightly,
she was bathed in the day's last warm breath.
It is hard to believe, but it wasn't until college
that I noticed the decapitated head Judith holds
in the shadows of the foreground.
I had always been focused on her.
I didn't see the beard, the eye, her hand
clenching his matted black hair.
The head of Holofernes held helpless, her
slice to his neck silencing the sound of
"You are not strong"
"You have no power"
"You're just
a woman"
I loved her more when I knew Judith killed.

She watches me now
from the wall behind the couch
in the living room of our farmhouse.
Holding his head, Judith pauses before she speaks to me
"I am still strong."
"I am still beauty."
"I am still power."
"I am still
you."
I look back to her
and always answer
"Yes."

Coffee Shop Somewhere on a Saturday Afternoon

…and we've decide to just forget the house and focus on our marriage. So what are you going to do now that you are home? Sleep. I don't mean to scare you but you know how those two guys are. Do you have soy milk? One other chair. We'll need one other chair. I'm sure you'll enjoy it more over here. Refill, please. I'm sure down the road it will be better. It's two hours! I'd rather take Saturday as a family day. Do you have silverware? Yep. Perfect. Take your time. Something threw me for a loop. I mean, I'm a woman. What's going on? Well, it was really great to meet you both. Her dad never wanted her to know about it. That's ok, we're just in a little bit of a hurry. Do you want us to just walk over there? It's like we have these minutes everyday. If you don't mind, we really don't have any change. We're just not sure. How are you feeling health wise? What made you decide to come here and join us? They took our plates! Oh! My coffee! Because they were just slabs the last time I saw them. Yeah, it happened a couple times. Did you have regular coffee? We were both on the same page. We both wanted to have a baby. But at the same time we didn't know if we wanted to spread that love to another child. Well it was working fine! I'm sorry. So we're just starting. How low? He so has that need to control. Where are you? Where are your priorities in life? It's like this wasn't supposed to happen. Well, she's always available. It's a rule. It's awkward. I can't stand it. Thanks for inviting him. It's happened, like, 15 times! Give yourself some credit. That's not a bad thought. You can do that and I'll just get in my car and leave. I was dressed. I was feelin' it. My husband never said to me everything is fine…

Snowed In

Winter

is a quiet

unlike

any other.

The air

rests

in my ears

like a sleeping

giant. Heavy,

silent and

much too still,

as if it will

wake

at any

moment,

open

its jaws,

and swallow

me whole.

February

She regretted having worn her parka.
Billowing and blue, it hovered around her
like the bell of a jellyfish as she shoveled
the crusted plow mound at the end of the driveway.

THIS is when it would be nice to have a roommate.

Two open houses on the block today—
all morning young couples holding hands,
dumb in love and real estate, traipsed between them
investigating parking options and bathroom sizes.
The men needlessly stylish in cashmere overcoats,
the girls squealing—high heels sinking deep in the new snow.

Who on Earth wears stilettos in February, in Wisconsin??

She glared, slung the dirty slush into the street, each throw splashing
freezing grey mush across the legs of her frost-bitten blue jeans.

If that chick fucking giggles like that one more time I swear to God...

She wondered if they would reconsider moving to the neighborhood
if they caught her icy eye between the heaping white peaks on the curb
or perhaps her next load of snow in their mortgaged faces.

Milwaukee

I remember sunrise in the city being lot more colorful.
Instead, the grey just lightened up and suddenly,

it was morning. The Findorff crane rests
for a moment, waiting for another beam.

Tiny white lights pour over the Hoan bridge
as I watch rush hour commence. Black coats

and pressed pants stride the sidewalk.
The crane spins back to starting position.

Over-stuffed packages are caught on the roof
of another building-in-process. It's actually

difficult to tell if the building is being built
or dismantled. But it's doubtful the city

would take so much care to undo a building.
One smokestack billows into the sky—

the smoke soon indistinguishable from the
grey morning. Street traffic picks up.

7:25 a.m. You need to be at work
in 35 minutes…or maybe 5.

Disquiet

Solar storms and stomachaches
feeding anxiety, encouraging mistakes.
Drawing anger out, shoveling worry in

every night's sleep seems to wake
as soon as it begins. Drenched in sweat,
I am boiled awake hours away

from a lucid state. My eyes snap open,
I hurl my covers aside and fumble
for my phone to check the time.

The unnatural blaze of cellular light
that we now completely accept
as just a part of our life informs me

that it's three in the morning—
Why the fuck am I awake?!
As usual, checking the phone was a mistake.

The luminescent rabbit hole that tempts
to trivial and text as we numbly type
and swipe to the next and the next.

I didn't have to look. What difference did it make?
I still wish I was sleeping and I'm still awake.
But these days, who still lies still in sleeplessness's dark embrace?

Who doesn't reach for their personal distraction database?
How have we arrived in this place where our eyes thirst
for screens and our hands are constantly occupied

by gleaming machines? This desire for answers
sooner than instantly, before immediately and
quicker than now has left us less able

to comprehend somehow that our addiction

to knowing is not as intelligent as it seems
as ideas give way to updates and devices replace dreams.

Mouth

I took one step

into the fog and

was dripping-thick

with night.

Your shadow

hovered

over my limbs

a soundless weight

in the haze. Air hung still

as love's lifeless body

in the corner

of our bedroom.

Your frame

eclipsed

the doorway.

My eyes

mined for light

in the night,

exposing the slow

billowing veil

of my breath.

I tried to remember

the language

that led me

to you.

I thought about

your

mouth.

The way it

moved

around

the

words

when

you

lied.

Hard,

hollow,

and cold—

your

voice

broke

like bone.

Nov 21, 2017
After the Inauguration

felt like cosmic debris,
noxious shrapnel,
and flaming tumbleweeds
rolling around in my skull.
The twisted wreckage of reason,
rubble of wisdom,
and ruined remains of grace
heaped against my soul's door

obstructing.

I still can't seem to shake this
constant barrage of garbage,
the spew and spray
of anger and hate,
the weight of indifference pushing
closer and closer,
deeper and deeper,
into my body
where the

grip of infection

can grab

and squeeze me
from
inside.

I breathe and stretch and try to

release

but it just
squeezes
me
harder.

I write and write and write
until something makes sense,
and yet,
     I can still
     feel it
     waiting
     for me.

          Its hot breath
          on my neck
          in the dark.

          I can't see it
          but I know
          it's reaching
          for

          me too.
               I feel it
               pull me
               in.

          I know it's not safe

               in there.

          But I
          can't seem
          to find
          the way

               out.

908 Days Later

It's still
not safe

       in there.

Since then,
my mother has defended
locker room talk.
My uncle has exclaimed accolades
to "Our boy Donny."
My cousin has given me
repeated side-eye eye rolls.

I have left more conversations
than I have been welcomed to.

                I have floated out to sea
                  with my husband,
                       my pen,
                  and a few other
           X-marked family members
       where we have weighed anchor
               to watch the shore
                smolder and seethe.

               The smoke fumes signal
          the impending aftermath,
           like frayed rope floating
            over feral waves.

Now,
I write and write and write
and the only thing that makes sense
is to persist
to resist
to insist
    on something better.

I can provide relief.

I can speak truth.

I can supply poetry.

I can write

    like life depends on it.

    Because it does.

    To bring

    something better

        in

    is the only way

                out.

Never Fell

Last night, I was Eve.
I wore spike heeled
snake-skinned boots.
My hair was short—
I was not the Lady Godiva Eve,
painted by so many ribs,
long, blonde, and naked.
My hair was red. My legs were long,
my tongue was longer.
Born by the piercing,
the consecration of metal
to flesh, of skin to skin.
I was forced from muscle,
swelled out of blood, tendons
and twisting tissue.
No bone bore me.
I walked into this world,
and I did not fall.
I made an entrance.
What shame should
make me want
to hide the soft glow
of my bare, buttery skin?
Should you not
look on me and see
the beauty that is
creation?
I will feed this hungry body.
I will lubricate my eager spirit.
I will not live
on a diet of deprivation
when fruit is bulging
from the branches
swollen with juice and
tender meat.
I will devour
what tries to devour me.

You will know me
by my outstretched hand.

To the 4 a.m. Light

When I opened my eyes
you were unexpected.
You,
a shimmering white square
draped over the edge of the bed
beside my akimbo limbs and
muted motion. A slumber-logged
body unaware and unprepared
for such a bright, defined light.
The only barrier between us
the shadow of my comforter,
a feather and warmth wall
separating your surprise
from my thighs.
I assume the moon is huge.
Full. Determined.
It's the only way you
could have cut through
the deep November night,
framed in my bedroom skylight.
You,
4 a.m. light,
brazen, bold, and bright,
drifting through the darkness
to my bedside.
In my sleep stupor,
I did not know
where you had come from,
only that you had come,
and would not leave
until morning shoved you
over the edge of the roof.
I closed my eyes and
imagined you
beneath the covers
lighting the places in me
too dark for anyone else to see.

Hydrangea

In December the white heads nodded to me
through the fractured kitchen window.
Ice-bound stalks bowed
beneath winter's weight and splayed
across the snow as though an
invisible cat had settled in their center.
January's white-out winds
sent blossoms flailing like
a clutch of wind-whipped balloons.
In February drifts mounted
against the garden fence,
confining the hydrangeas in
static soundlessness—the mute
white noise of immobilized air.
Now in the reach of Spring,
crisp brown globes balance
on rigid sun strengthened stems,
blossoms bob sleepily
beneath the first tepid rain.

Letter to Lake Michigan

We don't need to talk.
You always know why I need you.
You comfort without speaking.
You listen without hearing.
I know you will always forgive me.
When I wrap my arms around you
your embrace surrounds and slows me,
to the pace of sleep walking,
lifting the heaviness until I am floating,
concern sinking beyond my reach.
Your appetite for my troubles is always ravenous;
you swallow with each swell
the weight of my worry replacing the hollow
with currents of calm and comfort.
You have rendered me unable
to live beyond the reach
of a strong shoreline,
and incapable of inhabiting
a landscape without water.
Thank you.

Driving North

The snow surrounds like a static black hole
swallowing me as I knuckle the steering wheel.
The challenge of keeping my tires in the vanishing
tracks ahead puckers my body to the windshield
like an old woman—ever crooked forward
to get a better look at everything.
I veer over the tapering wedge of snow
that threads the median and feel
a skitter beneath me as my tires lose track.
I grip the wheel and mutter comfort to myself
as I coax my 1,800 pound battering ram from the brink
of icy misfortune, back into the caving tracks.
"Eaaaasy now, you've got this. "
I train my eyes to the edge of my headlights' sphere
and watch the white road rush toward me
barely able to distinguish which track
is passable and which has deepened.
I turn on my high beams. The snow explodes before me—
trajectory of each flake exposed in the glare,
flashing like out of control bullets,
miniature white rockets,
swarms of angry arctic fireflies.
I switch back to low beams and focus on my course.
I cannot tell how far I have gone,
or have yet to go, to reach my next turn.
The night teems with white, changing the perception
of darkness, canceling out depth of field,
making adjustment to night vision impossible.
Not that there would be much to see, even if I could.
But for once, I am not worried about deer in the road.
I know they are smart enough to stay home on a night like this.
I open my fists one at a time, extending fingers clenched
so tight to the wheel each joint feels like
hardened balls of granulated glue,
frozen pine sap,
coagulated molasses.
I roll my head side to side and stretch my neck.

Hours of attention through tension gather
at the summit of my spine and reach around my skull
encasing my eyeballs in a dry, papery ache.
I cannot think of anything but snow,
and yet, cannot think about it at all.
Each time I think *about* the driving snow
and not the act of driving *in* the snow,
I swerve
ever so slightly from my path and battle
the un-trekked swaths of snow that billow and growl
low loud moans of rubber skidding over ice beneath me.
Each groan punctures my confidence.
"Come on now, stay focused," I scold.
I catch a glimpse of my radio clock. 2:06 am.
The only other people on the road at this hour are leaving a bar.
Great. Just what I need. Some asshole to swerve up the tracks
I blindly follow and lead me into a ditch.
I concentrate on my objective.
The thought of the cabin soothes my nerves.
It's always better to wake up there,
even if it takes twice as long to arrive.
I turn the heat down and invite the cold air
to awaken my senses. The road looks less
like snow-covered ruins and more like
trampled cake frosting,
smashed mashed potato plaster,
unfurled frozen bed sheets.
I have come to the threshold of the last town to pass through
before I reach my destination. I relish the few miles
of compacted county-plowed snow
as I accelerate close to the actual speed limit,
then hunker down for the last 30 miles
of unplowed wilderness.

Cheers

I have decided.
I will stop being sorry
and I will start
drinking Scotch.

        Fuck tall, cool Tom Collins.
        To hell with wide eyed Martini trumpets.
        Screw that salty-rimmed Margarita, and
        damn that slim, trim white wine beaker!

I want rusty booze, an odd number of ice cubes,
in a short crouched glass—squat on the bar between
the pillar pints of beer and the snooty Brandy snifters.

Scotch on the rocks! Three fingers.
Who the hell was the first one to measure liquor in fingers anyway?
And why is a drink called "neat"
                     without ice?
There's nothing
         neat
            about it!
              I mean,
                    you still get that same soggy stain
             under your glass
                 on the napkin
                    on the bar.
                       But it helps me keep
                         track of my rounds…

Scotch! Rocks! Threefingers.

How did ice
            becooooome   *rocks?*

Was it the crunchcrack sound
        when bar temperature booze hit those cold bitches?
Or the way the sides smoothed
            when it melted

like rocks

        beaten by waves? The ice makes my drink sweat.
Leaves those damn soggy stains
under my glass
    on the napkin
      on the bar.

         Scotch! ROCKS!

You know,
    there's really   *noooooooothing* like a
    gooooood
      stroooong
        Sco-aahtch

To *beltyouinthemouthandknockyoubackintoshape!* HA!

                What do I have to be soooorry
aboutanyway?

You know,
measuring booze in fingers was a *genius*idea!

I just wish
    I had bigger hands…
           Heeeey!
             Hey! Look!
My fingers!
    are *bigger*
under my glass on my napkin on the bar!
           Hey!
             Lemme pour!!

Syncopation

We began as bluegrass.
Happily clattering
up and down tumbling
in and out of the sharp
spooling notes of newness.
Our bass was even,
a gentle thump like
soft shoes pacing grassless ground.
Our fingers fiddled
laughing and tickling the air
until we found sex's easy harmony.
We were simple. On time. In tune.
Drummed up and tightly strung
when the cadence changed.
Our strings began to snap Jazz
smooth, then swift
like the swinging current
of a dammed stream.
Our sporadic solos
suddenly sprung
out of low melodies
and wove between us
like amplified snakes
striking cymbal hisses,
our bodies composing a fantastic
cacophony of crashing
Percussion SnareBassTom
Screeching StringSongMic
Blasting TrumpetKeysSax
winds wailing,
bawling, pounding
music unplanned,
unwritten. We were
BrassDrumWood
StringMetalVoiceandSkin all
playing together.
No cords or rhythm,

we are all volume and noise.
Our coda
unmarked.

April

After an extended stillness,
motion comes slowly.
Warmth swells beneath
the surface, reminding limbs
what they were made for.
Each shuttered cloister of maple buds
shift inside their sanctuary
aching to part the folds
of their soft grey robes.
It is desire that drives this strain.
A want of transformation,
expansion beyond
the confinements of time
and temperature.
A need to awaken and expose
to light what has long been unlit.
The first bud to reveal
is often premature,
eager sap escaping
before the season allows.
A sticky beacon of protest
gleams in the early spring sun,
reflecting long-coveted
luminescence.
Such ambition. Such boldness
to grow before you have been fed.
Other enterprising organisms
follow your lead and
release themselves
to chance, hoping for
a well-timed deliverance.
Fine threads of flying seeds
careen on the breeze
to unknown homes,
unexpected ends. One
seed holds fast
to your sticky exposure,

interrupted by your fearlessness,
suspended
by your stubborn urge
for rebirth.

For Gerry

I've wanted to write you
a poem since you've been gone.
About how sometimes,
I forget you are dead.
How I goddamn you
when I remember.
How the truth comes rushing
back and blasts blizzards
through my veins.
About how I didn't
contact your Mom until
over a year after
your funeral. How
awkward it was
to have lunch with her
at your favorite Thai place.
How she told me what you
would have ordered and we
tried not to cry into our curry.
How I immediately regretted
my offer to help go through
the toppling boxes of your belongings
locked in your storage unit.   How
thankful I am that she still
has not asked for my help.
About how much I wish
I could bring you to my house
on the ridge surrounded by
tree-thick acreage and wild animals
and scare you silly by leading you
into the dark leafy uncertainty of the woods.
About how I heard coyotes howl
the night I started to write your epitaph
for the memorial brick being placed
in the new football stadium of our alma-mater.
How when we gathered on your birthday
to look at your little brick we had to

break into a building to find something
to shovel off the snow to see the damn thing. How I hoped
after that, I would not need to talk
to your Mom again. How the next time
I saw your Mom was at your girlfriend's wedding
to someone that is not you. How I could not turn
to look at your Mom during the ceremony
because I knew we shared
the same stupid thought, that it was
supposed to be you up there visibly
uncomfortable and sweating profusely
in a rented tuxedo. How I fled
to the elevator to someone's hotel room
to drink before the reception started.
How I did not visit your Mom at her table later,
or chat her up in that awkward time
between ceremony and reception.
About how I drank everything that night
and I reached the point when you realize
you are already screwed, so you might as well
just keep fucking drinking. How the next day,
I felt like I wanted to die. How I vomited
out the car window almost the entire
four hour ride home. How I never
wanted to drink again. How I was shameful
and overflowing with guilt and grief.
How I felt like a terrible waste of space, a needlessly
suffering asshole, a pile of shit being rained on
on the side of the freeway, an uncontrollable
addict sick with my own sick.
I've wanted to write you a poem.
But here we are.
Well,
here you were.

On The Day Before June

Dozens of bright blue damselflies
dart and hover over the pond.

Green and silver dragonflies tip and careen
from reed tip to lily pad. The twangy echo

of a bullfrog beneath the dock, a slight splash
where I am not watching. Breeze blows across

the pond, ripples folding and flooding over themselves.
Huge white clouds move steadily East,

bulbous bodies trembling in their wrinkled reflection.
I notice how quiet the dragonflies are.

Unlike the buzzing bees and dive-bombing flies,
the dragonflies cascade through the air

with barely a flutter sound, with wings
that gently whisper a cellophane crinkle.

I startle a slender snake from the marshy edge—
it's gone before I realize where it is going.

A yellow swallowtail butterfly glides overhead, then another.
They disappear on the breeze as quickly as they came.

Campsite #14

The last shadow of the mountain
looks like a hand
cupped to receive something small,
fragile. Everything else is purple.
The purple of bright pink
that has been tipped toward blue, then righted
at the actual shade
of the mountains' majesty.
The end of the daylight
on the tree-covered slopes glows
red, purple, orange.
The moon rises, swelling white in
the robin's egg sky.
All seems still at this
dusk except the
constant cackle of Slough Creek.
Returning to the mountains,
the shadow hand is still cupped
waiting to catch some tiny treasure.
Ah, Yellowstone,
how you restore me,
get me back to the truth.
How do I keep you
with me as I venture back into
the world of anger, politics, impatience,
greed, speed, and distraction?
I will take you with me. Bison, pronghorn,
sagebrush, thermophiles, geysers,
and the purple mountains' majesty.
Oh! Now, you are almost all shadow.
The shadow of the hand
reaches to receive
the shadow of the mountains.
Kingfishers chitter up and down the creek,
and now the mountains are grey,
glacier blue, like going back
to their beginning.

Revolutions

I want my hips
            to move like liquid
                        in the slippery
                                    curves of a chalice.
                                                Unbroken circles surging
                                                            hot hula hoop friction
                                                                        that rides the borders of bones,
                                                the slick of skin,
                                    the mountainous, mounting
                        tremor in my muscles
            that makes my mouth
open to an 'O' and cry out—
                        turning tides in
                                    and over and down and
                                                up and out and under and through
                                                            and around spit spiral spinning,
                                                weave whip whirling,
                                    twirl turn twisting
                        until my hot hip helix
            slows to tiny cork-
        screw swivels
slugging soft
        shallow circles
            until I can move no more
                        and my body skids
                                    to a stop slips
                                                and slides
                                                            sleepward
                                                                        smoothing the shiver
                                                                                    of spent muscle.

In the Afternoon

Only the leaves on the end
of the sumac branches move
when the breeze shoulders through.
The rest weave with their neighbors
into a tangled canopy of
wood and red and green.
When the end leaves meet and move,
it sounds like folded paper
edged by a fingernail
and torn along the seam.
A sound more made
than grown,
more paper than tree.
A chipmunk scuttles
in a tipped pickle bucket
then scales the woodpile.
She freezes as I turn to her,
tiny lungs heaving beneath her fury chest,
slender claws clenched
along the edge of a birch log.
She is temporarily paralyzed
in the moment between flee and freeze.
She darts,
then disappears beneath
rough-cut birch and willow
stacked like tumbled toy soldiers
at the bottom of the yard.

Short Avant-Garde Film

Fade in from image of a child's cowboy hat and spurred boots to interior of a bar.

Anonymous man seated in far right corner with his back to the camera
hunched over a poker machine.
Bartender in foreground wiping a glass
with a white towel.
Jack Kerouac seated directly across from bartender.

The bartender tells Jack Kerouac he does not serve top shelf alcohol.
Jack answers with some really profound statement
about it not really existing in the first place
and that there was no point in the bartender
telling him he couldn't have it because he already did.

Jack takes a shot of local whiskey
and places the empty glass upside down on the bar.
The bartender screws a cigarette into his lips
and walks to the opposite end of the bar.
Man in background gets up and exits the bar.
Fade to black.

Last shot of film reads:

Vision

+

Confidence

=

Art

I have a pile of cassette tapes to choose from for the soundtrack.
First, I pick Eric Burdon and War.
But then I think better of it
and chose Dave Brubeck Quartet's "Take Five".

Olfactory

It was something having to do with
a smell of coffee
or was it smoke?
Orange trees or
new rubber or
something much more
singular,
like a sweat-soaked
cloth-cord necklace
that strangled a chipped
Chinese character. (I never knew
its translation—maybe
Courage or *Magic*...
though *Caution*
would have been
more fitting.) A thick
sweet skin smell
that clung to the cord
and comforted,
until it revolted.
Or clothes that had
been lived in for
too many days
gripping a scent like wet,
like
almost sour,
like hiding.
It called to me
like a bakery or barbeque or
one of those stands
that sells cinnamon and sugar-coated nuts
shoveled hot into red-and-white-checked
paper cones. Like something
I knew better about.
It said
come closer
follow my veiled trail

until you are
right beside me.
And just try
not to breathe me
in deeper. Try
not to gasp and gulp
until you are filled
with rich rolling waves of
bittersweet burnt sugar,
the astringent sting
of menthol muscle salve,
the metallic inhale
of approaching snow.

Shore Lines

Beyond the dark cabin
the night waves shift.

The lake laps the beach
and rocks the rotting

dock posts, the low air
ripe with the weight

of wet wood. Seasoned
pier planks creak

like tired bones.
Fiddleheads and

foxtail curl beside
the spiny blossoms

of Indian Paint Brushes,
their silhouettes shaping

burst black firecrackers
that sway before the

last grey ribbon
of an aged day.

Fourth of July Family Reunion

Some of us felt oppressed.
Degraded, demolished by

the sheer weight of its being.
Others lay quietly beneath it

allowing themselves to be
covered in sticky thickness.

Many refused and refuged,
hiding behind tightly suctioned

doors and foggy windows.
Whatever way we coped, we knew

we had been swallowed by the
sticky, steamy heat of nearness.

Our flesh felt cumbersome, muscles
dead weight wrapped in boiled newspaper,

molten plastic, hot rotting meat.
Our skin kept a steady simmer,

a sour slick of sweat-wiping-sweat.
It didn't pay to attempt comfort

with fan or shade. The heat was
too determined. It saturated the shadows,

climbed on top of us, curled up in our
hair, squeezed beneath our fingernails,

and sucked like a parasite until nothing
was left but sticky and sweat.

It was hard to believe the flies could still
bite us through the sopping glaze

of dirt, sweat, and sunblock. But they could.
And they did. Each violent slap clapped

like lunchmeat on linoleum, each fly
escaping unscathed leaving behind

pin prick pain frustration
fuming in thick caramel heat.

Lunar Aptitude

Stereo frogs through the up
and downstairs windows-

the night sings songs
of summer across the still forest.

The waxing moon stark,
pinned to the sky like a medal

proclaiming to all who look
upon it the audacity

and courage that it takes
to be the fucking moon.

Turning tides and
shifting cycles, nobody

really understands
the pull and the power

of such a wild,
natural motion.

The sway she sustains
with the muses,

the clout she holds
with the calendar,

the sermon she speaks
to her nocturnal

congregation, the light
she holds back.

The One That Got Away

Fishing, you have hooked
the long elastic eye socket of my soul luring it
up and out of me. The amorphous bulk

bumps and scrapes against my internal angles
jerking limbs about as muscle rebels skin
and punches its way out. My head

reels back as your line tuned tight
casts my mouth wide and your hook pulls
the bruised hollow into unfamiliar light.

The eye swimming in the black stretch
of my soul's socket leaves a shiny liquid trail
as it is drawn out and over my lips.

The hook tears at the edges of the socket
and the eye starts to quiver.
Your reel buckles, lurches,

and the line snaps. Your catch flip-flops
over the deflated heap of me,
thumping gasps from the drained mass.

I close my eyes, open my mouth,
and invite my soul to slide back in,
before it runs out of breath.

I inhale until I feel the eye slick
on the back of my tongue,
and choke my soul back down.

It's tough to swallow something
that doesn't fit inside you.

An Offering Along the Menominee River

I wake to worship the day that has risen with me. Nothing
but the tight teeth of my tent zipper keeps me from receiving
the communion of morning. I coax the zipper over tender
spots of wear and open my mouth inviting the virgin air

to spread across my tongue and plunge into my lungs.
Placing my hands firmly on the ground I slide my body out
to enter the outside as it enters my insides. Naked knees
press on the menagerie of soil and seed. I am alone and only

in the early morning breeze. I am everything around me, I am roots
and rising trees. I stand and step, and step and stride, allowing
the riverbank to be my guide. My bare feet track over acorns
that feel like tiny bones, picking up pine pitch, affixing small stones.

I lift my eyes and gather light that does not yet know shadow.
Morning light, pure white, halo bright. There is no one here.
I am alone. I am light. I am free. I am clear. I am the only
singer of this psalm. I gather acorns and run my fingers over each

tracing continuous circles, learning the story of every seed. I repeat
their journey to myself until the words swell like wind and swim
through my bones, until they speak themselves in a low airy moan:
I grow. I live. I die. I grow. I grow. I live. I die. I grow. I live.

Softly fingering the rosary of nature, it is here that I practice
my religion. My undying devotion as I revel in the ecstasy of Earth.
I walk to the edge of the riverbank, hold myself steady, and close
my eyes. I release my vestments and reveal myself to the sky.

My body laid bare across sun-soaked rocks, I make an offering
to the day. The wind blesses my skin in places it has never been
and I begin to sway. I stand with my body against the current
as the air pours over me, like the tide over time,

like a wave I cannot catch. My body a dam in the breeze,
a rock in the stream of creation's soft breath.

Long Distance Postmark

Light cut
across
the room
like warm
fleshy knives
sinking
into my skin.
A feeling
too hot,
too much
like desire
and obsession
to shine
away the
sickness
that lived
beneath the
sheets, and fed
on my bones.
From millons
of miles away,
the sun
cooked me
in my own
juices.
I could
only imagine
how hot it
must have been
where you were.
You who was
living in sand
and lying in
letters.

The curls of
your script
averting
my eyes with
sweet swears
of how I was
the only word
in your mouth
the only tongue
on your skin
the only body
in your memory.
I sat steaming
over what I
did not know
when I did not sleep
why I did not see
your shadow
swell in the
lonesome light
pillaring the length
of the my
empty hallway.

But I was not
the only one
waiting for your
long distance
postmark.

P.S.
Years after I forgave you,
I found your letters.
and burned them all

in my backyard.
Watching the flames
consume the serpent twist
of your penmanship,
I smiled
and envelopes
became ashes.

On the Evening Before August

The soft nudge of a balmy summer breeze
draws out the swish of each
individual leaf caressing its neighbor.
Obstinate chipmunks chirp and dart
beneath the deck and down the ridge.
Only the tips of the trees are still sunlit,
all else begins to darn the shadows
that will soon clothe the night.
A cicada drones, quiets,
then swiftly draws its
sharp sword of sound back up
to pierce the forest's whisper.
A few mosquitos start to pester
the fringes of my consciousness.
The jagged tooth outline of maple against sky
looks like thick, dark lace. The golden hour light
softly covering the ferns.
My fingers become lazy, hands splaying
across the paper, wielding a pen
that suddenly feels heavy.
I melt between this last dusk of July
and August's syrup simmer,
beneath the heft of humidity,
and into the lush of a ripe
summer twilight. I tangle
in the ethereal rhythm of
the Hermit Thrush refrain
as it twists from the underbrush
bends below branches, and uncoils
into evening. I weave myself
into the thick knit of nocturne,
and tug at its threads.

Foggy Mountain Breakdown

banjo twangin' boots a-bangin'
straw hat wearin' pants a-tearin'
buckshot shootin' long grass chewin'

foot a-stompin' grits a-chompin'
wood floor slippin' overall rippin'
moonshine swillin' an' distillin'

big gap smilin' fingers flyin'
old man spittin' his 'backy grinnin'
like there 'aint no mind to mindin'

'bout his skin a-splittin' hair a-frizzin'
mud squishin' milk a-gettin' pony pettin'
wagon ridin' gin tub hidin'

hot shot tossin' one eye watchin'
o'er his youngest girl her blue eyes battin'
laughter cacklin' toes a-tappin' hands a-clappin'

skirt a-spinnin' ponytail swingin'
sweat a-drippin' straps a-slippin'
skin a-showin' to boys a-knowin'

their lips a-smackin' bodies thrashin'
words a-ramblin' hearts a-gamblin'
their cheek a-missin' lady kissin'

mouth a-blowin' jugs a-flowin'
whiskey drinkin' breath a-stinkin'
voices wailin' tempers flailin'
fists a-crashin' bottle smashin'

til the mornin' risin' sun a-shinin'
our heads a-hurtin' bellies churnin'
arms a-achin' legs a-shakin' eyes a-stingin' ears a-ringin'

but the whiskey 'aint dry 'n we still try 'n
sing 'long with that bathtub snarin' fiddle tearin'
guitar bangin' washboard clangin'

mandolin puckin' corn shuckin'
pulse runnin' ever lovin'
heart stoppin' no toppin'

back breakin' barn shakin'
Old Earl's Fast Hand
Dirty Devil Bluegrass Band

Outside Canyonlands

The wind heaves across hot red rocks, lifting
juniper, sage, and pinion branches like

rippling green eddies in a blood sea.
So quiet, the sound absorbed by rock

and filtered through sand. Tan and brown
lizards dodge and scurry from ledge shadow

to rock hole—toes and tails that move
without sound unlike our flat flopping feet,

that give us away with sand slides and
pebble cracks. You pour over maps

while I listen to the landscape. Both of us
plotting ourselves across the open land,

seekers in a naked terrain, travelers exposed.
Silent busts of stone perch atop skirts

of sand and debris that seem to crumble,
then regain composure into hoodoos—

columns of color and shadow remaining erect
amidst the rubble. Dusk reduces the desert boil

to simmer and I exhale, at last able to
handle the heat. Reclining in a rock nook,

I feel the power beneath the shelf of sunbaked
stone, heat possessed in windblown curves

and eroded crevices. After sunset, the moon
and stars ignite the desert white. We press

our bare skin into the shadows and brace
against the rocks. Sand and pebbles push

into my palms as you thrust me deeper
into our unseen alcove. The only

campers on this western flank
of Hamburger Rock Campground,

the sound of sand sliding beneath us
seems to echo across the open desert.

I arrest the gasps in my throat
before they betray our exertion.

Naked, seeking our terrain
we are travelers exposed.

Tomato Soup

Sitting alone in the Anaba Tea Room I thought I heard Andy Warhol
talking about spiritual growth behind a Grecian urn across the room.
Andy's voice was like spoiled milk, dribbling soft and thin, then sinking
like wet sand. I listened and thought about growth in neon colors.

I thought about life in ink smudges. I saw art in my cucumber sandwich.
I saw love in my jasmine pearl tea. I poured my tea and sloshed
two large splashes from the pot. I watched the stains dilate
on the paper placemat and seep to the bleach white table linen.

I leaned to peek around the urn and my eyes met a blinding beam. Light filtering
through the atrium ceiling shot a glare from beneath the baroque fountain
in the center of the room. I blinked and the shine shattered into infrared filigrees
following the course of thick green vines that fell from the garden room above.

Andy began to whisper. I wondered what he would have ordered had he
sat at my table. Soup of the day? Would he have been disappointed when it did not
come in a can? Was that what he meant by spiritual growth? The ability to desire
something so completely and outrageously that believing it will make it true?

I wondered if I was the only person who heard the voices of dead artists in tea
rooms. Would I hear someone else somewhere else? Was Marcel Duchamp
crouching behind the counter at Alterra Coffee Roasters? Would Gustav Klimt wait
for me in the discount wine section of Otto's Liquor? Did Edward Hopper

plan an encounter at Ma Fischer's All-Nite Diner? Shouldn't I
listen for them anyway? The tea had shriveled to splatters like pressed paper
raisins. I tilted my cup and wondered if it was odd that I did not finish my tea
so that I could watch the cloudy swirls mate in the bottom of the cup.

Andy spoke just below the volume of casual conversation
and I imagined myself at his table, listening to the serrated blade of his speech
saw through his truncated words. I watched the strands of his grey hair
separate and descend down the slope of his corrugated brow.

Behind the counter on the far wall, square smooth-edged glass canisters
stood nine wide, seven shelves high: Oolong, Chai, Darjeeling, Moroccan Mint,

Lemongrass Melange, Yerba, Silver Needle, Earl Grey, Pu-erh,
and Jamaican Red Bush. A transparent wall of tea, each blend heaped

a different level, shade, and intensity created an uneven Mondrian
to the right of Andy's head. I stared into his seedy eyes and wondered
if he was looking at me or through me. I panned my gaze
to search his face for a tell. Andy was quiet.

The round rims of his glasses stood out
like black condensation rings on the pale finish
of his face. Behind them his pupils looked calcified.
Andy's mouth gaped a little and I listened to him exhale

a long unbroken breath. I thought about where Andy
had been and where I was going. I wondered if
anyone who was not there had ever spoken to him.
I watched Andy's pale spider hand reach

across the table and stop just short of my fingertips.
I rose and imagined his steps shadowing mine across
the tiled tea room floor. I listened for the ceramic tap
of his black leather boot heels.

Through the Window of a Chicago Hotel

The city gives birth to an artificial sunset, the orange glow
shifting shades between shadows on the walls of our hotel room.
The sky has not moved—cake puzzles of clouds frozen above

the square steel stands protruding like buttons tempting a push.
The snow stopped, leaving the cold air to echo car horns
without the mute of temporary lace to soften them.

The night dim seeping in the light stands up and puffs
thin plumes—luminous feathers that extend as eyes squint
at bulbous gold street lamps. Red blinking hands. Florescent

white reflections. How many people can I see without seeing
in the stacked square windows grey with vacancy, or golden
with arrival? Sirens stretch like sour cats, sound bending unseen

through the streets. The clouds seem to blush from the crowding
heat of the city night. What was once expressionless grey,
is now purple and pink, skirted with violent violet-red as the skies bruise

over the city; subtle evidence of the injury beneath this battered skin.
So much sadness in cities brooding behind the calculated shifts
of our eyes over sorrows panhandling in our path, reminding us

of our own shortcomings and struggles. Or perhaps not.
Perhaps it's just that we refuse to acknowledge
that our lights and buildings and one-way-streets

and loading-zones-only don't give anything back
that's worth keeping, or away that's worth having.
It doesn't give us a connection, but a resistance to ourselves.

No true link to being part of the Earth, to learning how to feel new
in nature. It only exists here on private roof top terraces, and in
time-watered, seasonally-themed promenades. I wonder, do we realize?

Do we see? Do we know? Do we feel? Do we care about the lack
of relation? The inability of so many to feel the pulse of the planet, or the true
belt of the seasons as it tightens across our stride? In my search for the words,

the city has taken on the full cloak of night. The artificial light
in full command makes shadows for homeless to home behind
while we speed past punching our horns and ignoring our blind spots.

January Birds

Chickadees flash harlequin faces
as they skip and skitter
to the birdseed. Nuthatches fluff feathers,
careen their beaks backward

toward the recently-blued evening.
Nightfall renders the hues
of a Hopper-esque seascape,
a frightened pastel pallet shifting easily

as the dark of moisture closes in.
Downy woodpeckers slide their tufts
sideways across the bark
of the oft-grazed oak beside the feeder.

The snowy woods glow an ultra-violet blue
that is as stunning as it is unrecognizable,
irreconcilable in its tech-tone—though it is the true,
unaltered color of a mid-winter dusk

in the north woods of Wisconsin.
When the entire outdoors become blue,
the birds fly from the feeder
to their snug winter nests.

They know not even the boldest
song bird is spared by the
artic bite of this January evening.

Surveying the Damage

My largest piece of beach glass
holds pages open
in last night's reference book.

Only one mechanical pencil loaded,
the rest empty
as spent shotgun shells.

Batteries removed from my
desk clock, my frantic scribbles
tick across the page.

Poetry propped up beneath the halogen lamp,
a library book (*Writing about Writing*)
liberally notated:

tone

balance

object and image

poem in location to the reader

the structure of art   *image*

THINK about it Yes!

Language   *tension*   *distraction*

Aspects of tone   *process of discovery*

HOW?   *Balance*

Visual   *undercurrent*

the reader's desire to know

I read about writing
to write about writing
to read my writing
about writing
to write.

A Study in Topography

I know the height of every peak
and the depth of every canyon

so well that I could travel each
blind, feeling the territory.

I will map this terrain—
tracing lines over your breath

like long finger swipes on
frosted glass, reading the

compass rose of your eyelids.
Your drowsy limbs roll

slow waves of winter
over my body to my feet,

stray white quills of down
wisping in the yellow sheen

shining between the blinds.
I breathe quiet grey breaths

of morning and watch the early
light creep toward me like

luminescent caterpillars across
the summit of your back.

As you stir from sleep
the movement of your

waking body shifts
the landscape of our bed.

Letting it Out

After screaming at the cell phone, the computer, the tablet,
the television, the internet, all of the devices that keep

my photos caged, my files captive, my thoughts confined,
my words contained, I realize I must release myself.

I refuse to let my voice be trapped in tangled wires and
twisted cords. I want my voice to live in the leaves, to move

across the land, to rush like water and splash around rocks,
like an explosive, unstoppable wave. I want my voice

to weave between ferns and tumble in the breeze.
I want my voice to whisper the desert sands and bellow

down glaciers and mountains. I want nature to extract
the sound from deep inside me and shower it over

the fields and into the ground. I want my voice to make mud.
To lift wings with warmth and morph the clouds into visions

of approaching revelations and swelling, swirling fronts.
I want my voice to change the weather. And move the trees,

and roll the stones and bury old bones with moss
and hungry slugs. I want my voice to be natural.

To be full. To be courageous, and real and new
and growing. I want no wires. No buttons.

No switches. No lights, but the beam of the moon,
the blind of the sun, the bright of the morning,

the shine on the water. My voice lives
in the woods. Where it can spread out and sing

and whisper and call and shout and move.
My voice will not be kept inside.

Sleeping on the Third Floor

I was awoken by windows.
Wind raged into sills pressing
wooden lips to moan and
squeal splinters like ungreased

bows scraping out-of-tune strings.
Tempested air between the un-insulated
panes erupted spine searing cat fight
screeches, that speared from the night's

twisted symphony and reeled
above my bed, weaving a
warped soprano lace
that encased me like a

transparent coffin from sleep.
I lay watching my belly ascend
and entwine the eye of the web
until I was coiled into fine wire,

then spread thin to drape
over the headboard, hang
from the bedpost,
undulate in the wind.

Clarity

I am building a sacred place within my heart.
Building a space inside my own mind to be free
and place my energy into creation and light.

I am building a sacred place.

Sometimes I struggle and suffer and sabotage.
Sometimes this cavernous yearn for fullness challenges.
Yet, I continue to smile and exist and believe
that something good is there. That all things are truly possible
if I can withstand the judgment of my own mind against myself.

I am building a sacred place within my heart.

I have the power, if I so choose to exercise. To let myself
be happy while continuing within the discomfort
and discouragement of the challenges of living towards fulfillment.

I am building a space inside my own mind to be free.

It is difficult at times to stand up to the negativity and doubt
brought on often by those who do not strive, but even
by those to whom I am the closest that love the most.
But it is I who allows myself to be deflated from joy
by these carefully doubting elements.

I am building a space to place my energy in creation and light.

How do I begin to achieve and realize without the ability
to see what I desire exist? If I do not allow myself to dream
or believe in what I seek, how will I ever find it?

I must recognize, respect my own passion and seek
and follow and pioneer my path. This is instrumental
in happiness, joy, contentment, and fulfillment.

Visualize.
Intention.
Believe.
Build.
Arrive.

I am building.

Acknowledgements

I would like to acknowledge the following publications and/or exhibits in which several of these poems were featured:

the Aurorean "Hydrangea"

Stoneboat Literary Journal "Ticket Stub"

Puff Puff Poetry, Prose and A Play "Cheers" and "Morning"

Uncommon Core: Contemporary Poems for Learning and Living "Never Fell"

Wisconsin DNR's Wisconsin's Great Lakes Calendar "Letter to Lake Michigan"

Minerva Rising "Never Fell"

straightforwardpoetry.wordpress.com "Apology"

John Michael Kohler Arts Center's Wordplay Exhibit "Coffee Shop Somewhere on a Saturday Afternoon"

Stonecoast Lines: Volume II—"Surveying the Damage"

I would also like to thank the many generous souls in my life who have supported me and my work with faith, encouragement, constructive criticism, and love:

Anthony, Gina, Meghan, Tealeaf, Beth, and Kayni. Tim, Baron, Gray, Laurie, and Fr. Neilson. Brianna, Sara, Brooke, Kelly, Heather, Stephanie, and Erin. Luke, Bob, and Austin. Eric, Avarie, Rox, and Olivia. Vickie, Rich, Kimberly, Shawn, Mitch, and Amy. Cath, Nancy, and Wendy. Lois, Grandma, Dad, Mom, Andrew and Morgan.

THANK YOU!!

Thank you Derrick for pushing me to the page when I need a shove.

And thank you Ms. Bolle for giving me Joyce and seeing potential.

Adrienne S. Wallner spent two years as an AmeriCorps Youth Advocate and Outreach Worker at a non-profit runaway and homeless prevention program where she worked with at-risk and incarcerated youth, teaching a variety of skills including creative writing, journaling, anger management, and healthy habits. After three years teaching Expository and Persuasive Writing at a liberal arts college, she felt called to continue working with at-risk youth...in the wilderness. Adrienne then began her most challenging and rewarding work as a Wilderness Instructor at an outdoor immersion therapy/education program. During her 8-day shifts, she camped and hiked in the Chequamegnon-Nicolet National Forest of Wisconsin, year-round, with at-risk and trauma-affected teens. Here, she witnessed first-hand the healing power of nature, the incredible strength of the human spirit, and immense gratitude for the gift of having one's basic needs met. Though incredible work, Adrienne eventually had to transition into a new adventure. A short stint as Lifestyle Editor at a newspaper later, she and her husband Derrick realized a shared dream and became National Park Rangers. Adrienne and Derrick moved to South Dakota and spent the summer of 2016 teaching visitors about Mount Rushmore National Memorial. After a road trip with the goal of hitting has many NPS sites as they could during the 2016 Centennial celebration of the National Park Service (72), the travelers made their way home. Adrienne returned to the non-profit world and began writing, marketing, and teaching for a non-profit arts center in northern Wisconsin. Originally from the Milwaukee area, she now lives in the north woods of Wisconsin where she writes and works as a contract grant writer. Adrienne's poetry has been nominated for a Pushcart Prize and can be found in *Straight Forward Poetry, Uncommon Core: Contemporary Poems for Learning and Living, Minerva Rising, Stoneboat Literary Journal, New Verse News,* and *Puff Puff Poetry, Prose and A Play*. She earned a B.A. in English with an emphasis in Creative Writing from St. Norbert College and a M.F.A. in Creative Writing with an emphasis in Poetry from the University of Southern Maine—Stonecoast. Adrienne loves hula hooping, hiking, music, classic cinema, taking photographs, and spending time near, on, and in water.

CPSIA information can be obtained
at www.ICGtesting.com
Printed in the USA
FSHW010903060421